SOMERVILLE

D1210710

FEARSOME
REPTILES

Camilla de la Bédoyère

QEB Publishing

Created for QEB Publishing by Tall Tree Ltd
www.talltreebooks.co.uk
Editors: Jon Richards and Rob Colson
Designer: Jonathan Vipond
Illustration pp18–19:
Mick Posen/www.the-art-agency.co.uk

Copyright © QEB Publishing, Inc. 2012

Published in the United States by
QEB Publishing, Inc.
3 Wrigley, Suite A
Irvine, CA 92618

www.qed-publishing.co.uk

All rights reserved. No part of this publication
may be reproduced, stored in a retrieval system,
or transmitted in any form or by any means,
electronic, mechanical, photocopying, recording,
or otherwise, without the prior permission of the
publisher, nor be otherwise circulated in any form
of binding or cover other than that in which it is
published and without a similar condition being
imposed on the subsequent purchaser.

A CIP record for this book is available from the
Library of Congress.

ISBN 978 1 60992 281 8

Printed in China

Picture credits
(t=top, b=bottom, l=left, r=right, c=center, fc=front cover,
bc=back cover)
Alamy 12–13 David Fleetham, 17t Allstar Picture Library;
Corbis fc Jack Goldfarb/Design Pics, 24–25 W Perry
Conway; **FLPA** bctr ZSSD/Minden Pictures, 26–27 Pete
Oxford/Minden Pictures; **Getty Images** 12–13 AFP, 20
Visuals Unlimited, Inc./Michael Kern, 22–23 Pete Oxford;
Nature Picture Library 7b Michael D. Kern, 17b Barry
Mansell, 21t Michael D Kern; **NHPA** bctl Martin Harvey,
1 Woodfall Wild Images/Photoshot, 2–3 Daniel Heuclin,
4–5 Ken Griffiths, 5 Photoshot, 6 E Hanumantha Rao,
13 Martin Harvey, 14–15 Larry Ditto, 16 Mark Conlin, 22b
Martin Wendler, 27b Daniel Heuclin, 28–29 T Kitchen & V
Hurst, 29t Image Quest 3D, 30–31 Daniel Heuclin, 31b
Stephen Dalton; **Shutterstock** bcb Johan_R; **SPL** 9b Steve
Gschmeissner, 10–11 Matthew Oldfield, 11b WK Fletcher,
15 Ken M Highfill, 25b Nature's Images, 33 Nature's Images

Web site information is correct at time of going to press.
However, the publishers cannot accept liability for any
information or links found on any Internet sites,
including third-party web sites.

Words in **bold** are explained
in the Glossary on page 32.

HOW SCARY?

Look for this rating.
It will tell you how
scary each reptile is.

1—a little scary

2—pretty scary

3—scary

4—QUICK! RUN AWAY!

5—YIKES! TOO LATE!

CONTENTS

Actual size!

Check out this puff adder on page 30

TAIPAN

KILLER FACT

A taipan has enough venom to kill 250,000 mice, 150,000 rats— or 100 people!

Snakes are smooth-scaled, slithering **predators**. These reptiles have speed and super senses, and some can inject a deadly **venom** using their fearsome **fangs**.

The taipan is also called the "fierce snake."

The deadly taipan lives in Australian deserts and is the most venomous snake in the world. Taipans belong to a group of snakes that are called elapids.

Like most snakes, taipans hunt small animals to eat, even entering their burrows. They only attack people if they are feeling scared.

A Quick Death

Most elapids are fast-moving snakes that can strike with lightning speed. When elapid snakes bite their **prey**, venom runs down grooves on a fang's surface or through a canal in the center of each fang. The venom usually affects the victim's **nervous system**, so it cannot move or breathe.

Taipans have needlelike fangs at the fronts of their mouths.

REPTILE BITES

Length: 12 ft. (3.7 m)

Habitat: Forests, deserts, and grassland

Where: Northern Australia

Weapons: Needlesharp fangs with deadly venom

HOW SCARY?

KING COBRA

A king cobra puffs out its hood when threatened to make itself look bigger.

The king cobra is the longest of all venomous snakes, and can reach a length of more than 16 feet (5 m). It's so big, a king cobra can raise enough of its body off the ground to look a human in the eye!

As hunters, king cobras have powerful venom and size on their side, but they prey on other snakes, not people. When they are scared, these snakes rear up, spread out their hoods, and hiss. Putting on this scary show is a type of defense and it should make most enemies think twice before coming any closer.

REPTILE BITES

Length: 16 ft. (5 m)

Habitat: Forests, grassland, and scrubland

Where: Southeast Asia

Weapons: Fangs with deadly venom

HOW SCARY?

KiLLER FACT

King cobras rarely kill people, but Indian cobras attack at least 10,000 people every year in India alone.

Mamba!

Everyone in Africa knows to look out for this snake, which is one of the world's most dangerous predators. Mambas can slither faster than a person can run, are active during daytime, and have a deadly bite. Thankfully, mambas normally hunt birds and small animals—not people.

Actual size!

One bite from a mamba can kill an adult human in minutes.

KOMODO DRAGON

KILLER FACT
Komodo Island has become a huge wildlife park where the dragons are protected.

REPTILE BITES

Length: 9.8 ft. (3 m)

Habitat: Scrubland and grassland

Where: Komodo Island, Indonesia

Weapons: Big claws and a venomous bite

HOW SCARY?

Few predators are more fascinating than the Komodo dragon. These huge reptiles rule the island of Komodo in Indonesia, but there are fewer than 5,000 of them left in the wild.

Komodos were not discovered until about 100 years ago.

Komodos are the world's heaviest lizards, and a male can weigh more than an adult human. They have strength rather than speed, and lie in wait for passing prey to **ambush** it. Komodos aren't fussy and will eat almost anything they find, including deer, pigs,— and even humans!

Deadly Bite

When a Komodo spots its prey, it springs to action and uses its sharp claws to hold the animal down. A quick bite with its sharp teeth allows the Komodo to pass venom into the prey's body. The injured animal runs away, but will soon weaken from its wound. The Komodo can then stroll over and finish its meal.

One side of a Komodo's teeth has jagged **serrations**.

SEA SNAKE

Sea snakes are venomous snakes that have taken to living and hunting underwater. Some sea snakes give birth to live baby snakes in water, while others come onto land to lay their eggs. They all have to come to the surface to breathe.

KILLER FACT
Sea snakes are known for their mild tempers, and it is very difficult to make one angry enough to bite.

REPTILE BITES

Length: 43 in. (110 cm)

Habitat: Shallow ocean water

Where: Pacific and Indian Oceans, Arabian Gulf

Weapons: Fangs with a muscle-eating venom

HOW SCARY?

Sea snakes have more powerful venom than any other snakes, but they rarely bite people and have small fangs. Sea snakes feed on small fish and mollusks.

If they do bite, sea snakes inject only a tiny amount of venom and their victims may not even know they have been bitten at first. The venom causes muscles to break down, and death can occur in a few hours.

Sea snakes swim slowly along the ocean floor looking for prey.

Land and Sea

Sea snakes called kraits come ashore to **shed** their old skins, to mate, and to lay their eggs. The females lay three to 10 eggs in old burrows left by seabirds or under rocks.

Like all snakes, kraits live alone, only coming together to mate.

SALTWATER CROCODILE

When the world's largest reptile decides it is hungry, no one is safe. The saltwater crocodile, or "saltie," is a fearsome hunter that uses **stealth**, speed, and strength to kill.

REPTILE BITES

Length: 8.2–23 ft. (2.5–7 m)

Habitat: Coasts, mangrove swamps, rivers, and lakes

Where: Southeast Asia to Australia

Weapons: 64–68 teeth

HOW SCARY?

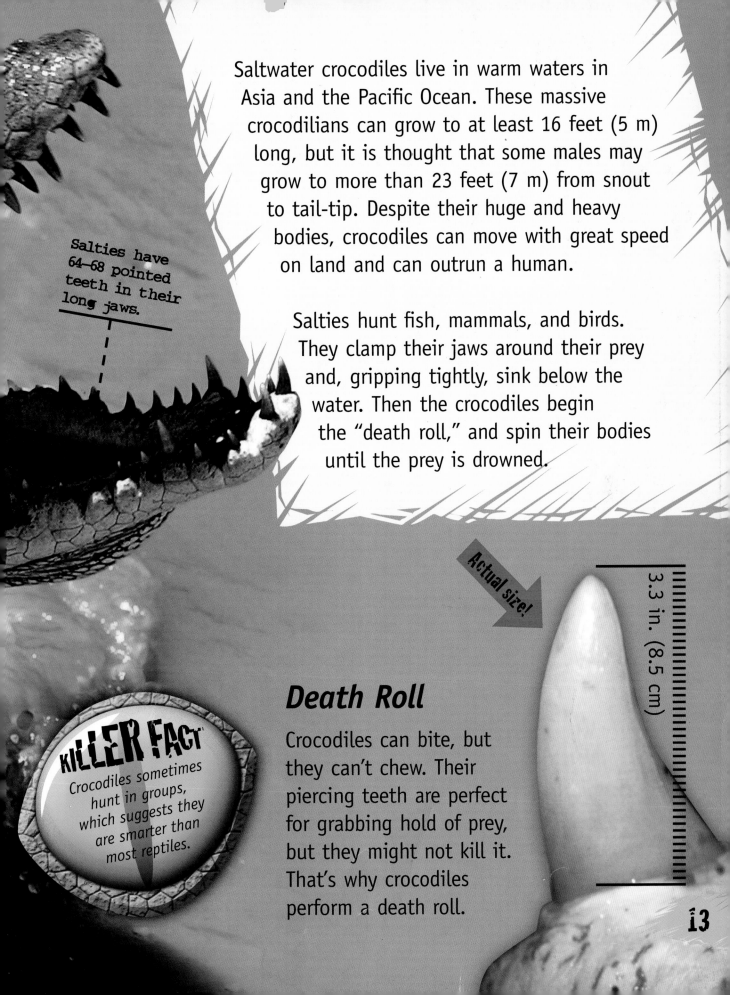

Saltwater crocodiles live in warm waters in Asia and the Pacific Ocean. These massive crocodilians can grow to at least 16 feet (5 m) long, but it is thought that some males may grow to more than 23 feet (7 m) from snout to tail-tip. Despite their huge and heavy bodies, crocodiles can move with great speed on land and can outrun a human.

Salties hunt fish, mammals, and birds. They clamp their jaws around their prey and, gripping tightly, sink below the water. Then the crocodiles begin the "death roll," and spin their bodies until the prey is drowned.

Salties have 64–68 pointed teeth in their long jaws.

Actual size!

3.3 in. (8.5 cm)

Death Roll

Crocodiles can bite, but they can't chew. Their piercing teeth are perfect for grabbing hold of prey, but they might not kill it. That's why crocodiles perform a death roll.

KILLER FACT

Crocodiles sometimes hunt in groups, which suggests they are smarter than most reptiles.

CORAL SNAKE

Coral snakes hunt lizards, snakes, frogs, nesting birds, and small mammals.

Look at the two snakes shown on these pages. Can you tell the difference? The coral snake in the main picture has red and yellow bands that warn predators of its venomous bite, but the milk snake opposite is a harmless copycat.

REPTILE BITES

Length: 35 in. (90 cm)

Habitat: Forests

Where: The Americas

Weapons: Fangs with deadly venom

HOW SCARY?

The yellow bands on this snake's body are next to the red color. This means it is a deadly coral snake.

KILLER FACT

Coral snake venom stops nerves and muscles working. **Antivenoms** often save lives.

There are about 40 different types of coral snake, with different patterns of colored bands. Most live in burrows and only come out at night, so humans rarely encounter these venomous creatures.

Coral snakes need to keep jabbing at a victim to inject all their venom, so although the venom is deadly in large amounts, it is rare for people to die following an attack.

Smart Mimic

Milk snakes can bite, but they don't have venom. Their cunning disguise, however, makes them look like venomous coral snakes so predators stay away. A rhyme helps identify some of these colorful snakes: *If red touches yellow, it can kill a fellow, if red touches black, it's a friend of Jack.*

ALLIGATOR

American alligators were so heavily hunted by humans for their skins, that they were in danger of dying out completely. Today, these impressive predators are protected.

This alligator is hiding under the algae, waiting for unsuspecting prey to pass by.

KILLER FACT
Although they breathe air, alligators can stay underwater for up to six hours at a time.

Like other reptiles, alligators need to keep warm to move at speed, so they spend most of the day floating in water and **basking** in the sun. When they float, alligators can stay almost completely motionless. Just their eyes and the tips of their noses poke above the water—looking for prey and smelling the air.

TURN THE PAGE TO GET UP–CLOSE TO A **DEADLY ALLIGATOR!**

Smaller young alligators often gather together in large groups.

Actual size!

Baby alligators are just 8.7 in. (22 cm) long when they hatch.

Taking Care

Female alligators build huge nests and lay about 45 eggs at a time. After the baby alligators hatch, their mother carefully lifts them in her mouth and takes each one down to the water.

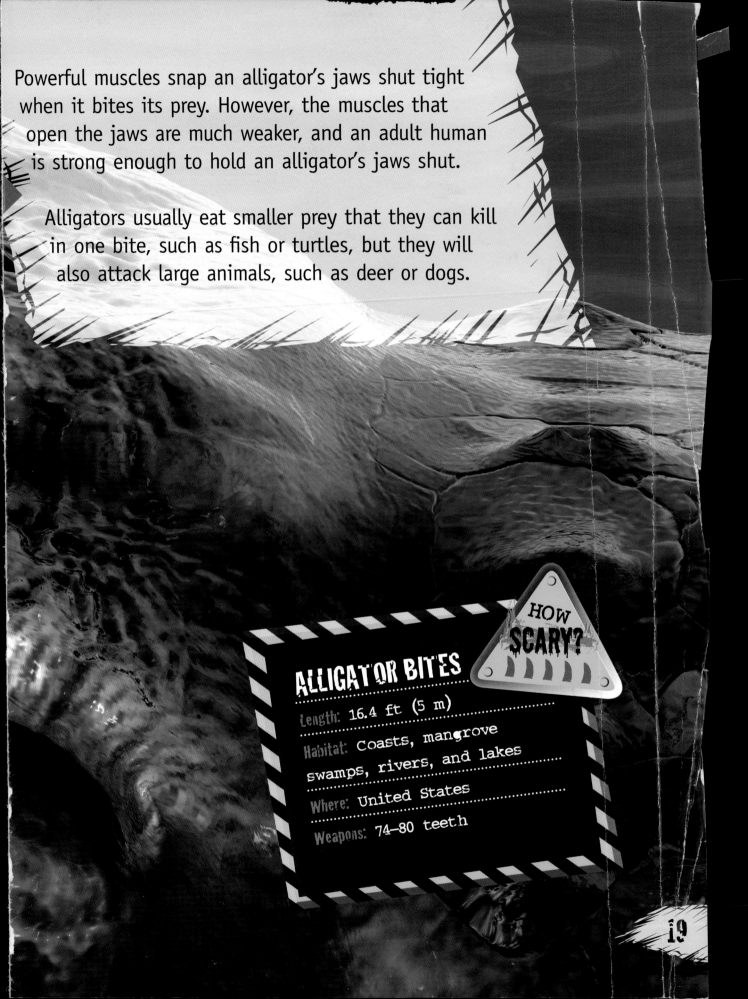

Powerful muscles snap an alligator's jaws shut tight when it bites its prey. However, the muscles that open the jaws are much weaker, and an adult human is strong enough to hold an alligator's jaws shut.

Alligators usually eat smaller prey that they can kill in one bite, such as fish or turtles, but they will also attack large animals, such as deer or dogs.

ALLIGATOR BITES

HOW SCARY?

Length: 16.4 ft (5 m)

Habitat: Coasts, mangrove swamps, rivers, and lakes

Where: United States

Weapons: 74–80 teeth

Actual size!

GILA MONSTER

Gila monsters move slowly, so they pose very little risk to humans.

These lizards are called monsters for a good reason—they have venomous bites. Gila monsters mostly use their venom to defend themselves from other animals.

Gilas are slow-moving desert lizards that prey on birds' eggs and bugs. Like other reptiles, these lizards can use their tongues to sense if food is around. When they flick their tongues, they are "tasting" the air.

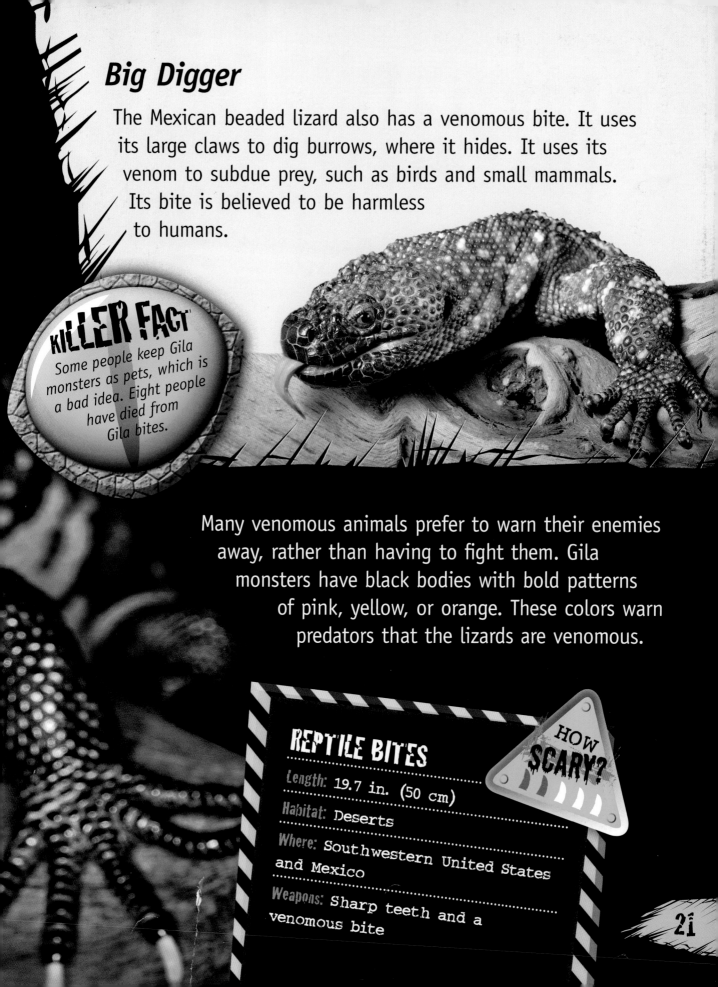

Big Digger

The Mexican beaded lizard also has a venomous bite. It uses its large claws to dig burrows, where it hides. It uses its venom to subdue prey, such as birds and small mammals. Its bite is believed to be harmless to humans.

KILLER FACT
Some people keep Gila monsters as pets, which is a bad idea. Eight people have died from Gila bites.

Many venomous animals prefer to warn their enemies away, rather than having to fight them. Gila monsters have black bodies with bold patterns of pink, yellow, or orange. These colors warn predators that the lizards are venomous.

REPTILE BITES

Length: 19.7 in. (50 cm)

Habitat: Deserts

Where: Southwestern United States and Mexico

Weapons: Sharp teeth and a venomous bite

HOW SCARY?

ANACONDA

Some fearsome reptiles take life at a slow pace, only stirring into action when hunger strikes. The **constrictor** snakes may survive for several months on one big meal!

Pythons and boas don't use deadly venom to kill their prey—they squeeze them to death instead. Anacondas are a type of boa. They spend most of their lives in water, but slither onto land to hunt. They ambush animals that come to the water to drink, grabbing them in their coils.

Anacondas wrap themselves around their prey and squeeze until it **suffocates**.

KiLLER FACT

Anacondas don't lay eggs. They give birth to up to 80 young snakes at a time.

A large anaconda is heavier than an adult human.

Massive Monsters

Anacondas are big enough to prey on large animals, including caimans, deer, and even people. A record-breaking anaconda measured 27.7 feet (8.4 m) long—as long as the net on a tennis court—and 43 inches (110 cm) around its middle.

REPTILE BITES

Length: 28 ft. (8.5 m)

Habitat: Rain forests, grasslands, and rivers

Where: South America

Weapons: Constricting coils

HOW **SCARY?**

23

BLACK CAIMAN

When caiman are underwater, special flaps close over their nostrils and ears to stop water from getting in.

Caimans are members of the crocodile and alligator family. Although they are great predators themselves, some types of caiman are close to extinction because humans hunt them for their skins.

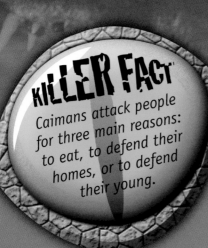

KILLER FACT

Caimans attack people for three main reasons: to eat, to defend their homes, or to defend their young.

Caimans use their excellent eyesight and sense of smell to hunt fish, waterbirds, and turtles. They spend most of the day floating in water, but when they come ashore at night, they may hunt mammals, especially **capybaras**, dogs, pigs, and deer. They have been known to attack people.

REPTILE BITES

HOW SCARY?

Length: 19.7 ft. (6 m)

Habitat: Rivers and lakes

Where: South America

Weapons: Sharp teeth

The black caiman is the largest predator in the Amazon rain forest

Head is 2–3 in. (6–8 cm) long

Actual size!

Caring Mother

Female black caimans lay up to 60 eggs in a nest near slow-flowing water. They stay on their nest to protect their eggs from predators, and take care of the babies after they **hatch.**

RATTLESNAKE

If you hear the distinctive noise of a rattlesnake shaking its tail, you know it's time to escape—fast! These are supreme hunting serpents with speed, strength, and some unbelievable superskills.

Actual size!

The snake's rattle is at the end of its tail

Rattlesnakes spend most of the day sunbathing, or hiding under rocks and in burrows. They hunt at dusk, when small mammals come out to find food, and can strike with amazing speed.

REPTILE BITES

Length: Up to 6.6 ft. (2 m)

Habitat: Deserts, mountains, and scrubland

Where: Southern USA and Mexico

Weapons: Long, hinged fangs, and venom

HOW SCARY?

When a snake flicks its tongue, it is smelling and tasting the air. When the snake pulls its tongue back into its mouth, it senses the smell using a special organ in the roof of its mouth.

KiLLER FAct

The Western diamondback is the most dangerous of all rattlesnakes, and its bites can prove deadly to humans.

Seeing in the Dark

Rattlesnakes can hunt in total darkness. They use special heat-detecting pits to find small animals. This super sense helps the snake to build up a picture of where an animal is, its size, shape, and even its movements.

Heat-detecting pit

27

ALLIGATOR SNAPPING TURTLE

This reptilian predator lurks beneath the murky water in swamps. When it lifts its ugly, scaly head above the water, the bad-tempered animal snaps its jaws and does a great impression of a prehistoric monster.

Alligator snapping turtles have one of the nastiest bites of any animal. They grow large and heavy, and live in fresh water where they feed on fish. Snapping turtles can reach the age of 100 or more.

With their spiked shells, these reptiles are known as the dinosaurs of the turtle world.

REPTILE BITES

Length: 31.5 in. (80 cm)

Habitat: Lakes, rivers, and swamps

Where: Southeastern USA

Weapons: Scissor-sharp jaws and a vicious bite

HOW SCARY?

Not What It Seems!

When a fish approaches a little red, wriggling worm, it has no idea it is swimming into the jaws of death. For that is no worm, but a lure— a wormlike lump of flesh inside the turtle's mouth that tempts fish and frogs to come close—SNAP!

KiLLER FACT

When the turtle sees food, it fills its lure with blood so that it looks red, plump, and very tasty!

PUFF ADDER

The body is thick, with a **girth** of up to 16 in. (40 cm).

When a puff adder is feeling scared, it puffs out its body to make itself look larger and hisses. But this snake has little to fear from anyone—it is one of Africa's deadliest snakes.

KILLER FACT
Puff adders are responsible for nearly two-thirds of all snakebites in Africa.

Puff adders are the most common snakes in Africa, and often live close to humans. They kill more people in Africa than any other kind of snake.

The pattern on its skin keeps the snake well hidden.

REPTILE BITES

Length: 39 in. (100 cm)

Habitat: Grassland and scrubland

Where: Central and southern Africa

Weapons: Ambushing skills, enormous fangs, and deadly venom

HOW
SCARY?

Hiding

With brown and cream **camouflage**, puff adders can hide in the undergrowth, waiting to ambush small animals. Their large, heavy bodies slither silently between plants, but when prey is close, these cumbersome snakes turn into speedy hunters. If they encounter a human, puff adders can easily deliver enough venom to kill.

A puff adder's long fangs can pierce leather!

GLOSSARY

ambush
A surprise attack made by an animal that has been lying hidden from view.

antivenom
A medicine that destroys deadly venom in a person's body.

basking
Lying in a warm place, such as sunlight, in order to get warm.

camouflage
A pattern of colors on an animal's body that hides it from predators or prey.

capybara
A large rodent that lives in the grasslands of South America.

constrictor
A kind of snake that kills its prey by squeezing it to death.

fangs
Long, pointed teeth that animals use for biting and tearing flesh.

girth
The distance around a body. The thicker its body, the bigger its girth.

hatch
The breaking out of a baby animal from its egg.

nervous system
A network of nerve cells in an animal's body that carries signals to and from the brain.

predators
Animals that hunt other animals to eat.

prey
Animals that are hunted by predators.

serrations
A series of sharp points that make a sawlike cutting edge.

shed
To take off the outer layer of skin. Snakes shed their skin as they grow.

stealth
Moving carefully and quietly in order to sneak up on prey.

suffocate
To die due to lack of oxygen, caused by not being able to breathe.

venom
A harmful substance that an animal injects into its victim's body by biting or stinging.

TAKING IT FURTHER

What makes a reptile "scary?" Now it's time for you to decide.

- Choose five scary features, such as speed, size, or weapons (such as teeth, claws, or jaws) and special powers (such as venom or camouflage).

- Use this book and the internet to award up to five points for each of a reptile's scary features. Repeat for as many reptiles as you want.

- Turn your results into a table, graph, or chart. Add up the totals to get a "Fearsome Factor" for each reptile.

USEFUL WEB SITES

crocodilian.com
Plenty of information on crocodiles, alligators, and caimans.

www.reptilegardens.com
An introduction to reptiles of all types and sizes.

www.sciencenewsforkids.org
For the latest exciting news on science from around the world.

www.defenders.org
Essential information on endangered animals, including reptiles.

TOP 5 DEADLY REPTILE FACTS!

> Spitting cobras blind their victims by spraying venom.

> Some prehistoric snakes were as long as a bus and as heavy as a car.

> Horned lizards defend themselves by squirting blood from their eyes.

> Some crocodiles can gallop, chasing their prey at up to 11 miles (17 km) per hour.

> About 2.5 million people are bitten by snakes every year.

INDEX